W9-BEM-302

THE PARABLES

The Lost Sheep

Luke 15: 3–7

RETOLD BY MARY BERENDES · ILLUSTRATED BY ROBERT SQUIER

Distributed by The Child's World®
1980 Lookout Drive • Mankato, MN 56003-1705
800-599-READ • www.childsworld.com

ACKNOWLEDGMENTS
The Child's World®: Mary Berendes, Publishing Director
The Design Lab: Art Direction and Design
Red Line Editorial: Contributing Editor
Natalie Mortensen: Contributing Editor

LIBRARY OF CONGRESS CATALOGING-IN-PUBLICATION DATA
Berendes, Mary.
  The lost sheep / by Mary Berendes; illustrated by Robert Squier.
      p. cm.
  ISBN 978-1-60954-392-1 (library reinforced: alk. paper)
  1. Lost sheep (Parable)—Juvenile literature. 2. Bible stories, English—
N.T. Luke—Juvenile literature. I. Squier, Robert, ill. II. Title.
  BT378.L6B47 2011
  226.8'09505—dc22   2011004957

Printed in the United States of America in Mankato, Minnesota.
July 2011
PA02087

The parables of the Bible are simple, easy-to-remember stories that Jesus told. Even though the stories are simple, they have deeper meanings.

One bright day, a crowd gathered around Jesus. He told them this story:

———

A kind shepherd stood watching over his flock. He had 100 sheep for which he cared greatly. Every day he watched over them and protected them. He made sure they were always safe.

One day, a sheep left the shepherd's flock. It wandered over hills and rocks. It wandered through forests and fields. Soon, the sheep was lost.

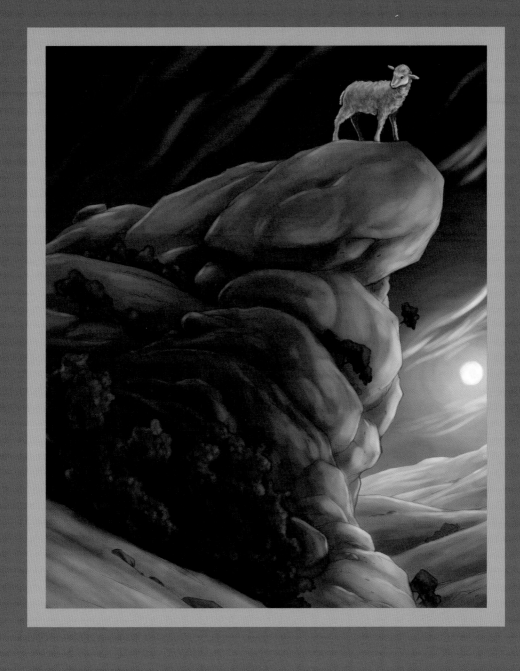

As night grew near, the shepherd noticed that one of his sheep was missing. He knew the poor sheep would be cold and afraid. But he could not leave the other 99 sheep all alone while he searched for the missing sheep...could he?

The shepherd decided to leave the other sheep and search for the lost one. He looked under bushes and into dark caves. He searched thick forests and fields. At last, he heard the frightened sheep calling out. Baaa! Baaa!

The shepherd ran to his lost
sheep. How happy he was!
He picked up the sheep and
carried it all the way back to
the flock.

The shepherd then called to his friends. "Come and celebrate with me, for I have found my lost sheep!" The shepherd's friends did not understand.

"Why are you so happy that you found one sheep?" asked one friend. "You should be happier that the other 99 sheep didn't wander off." The shepherd just smiled and hugged his lost sheep. He was too happy to let his friends' words bother him.

"The kind shepherd is very
much like God," Jesus said to
the crowd. "God is happiest
with a sinner who changes
his or her ways than with
99 people who don't need
God's help."

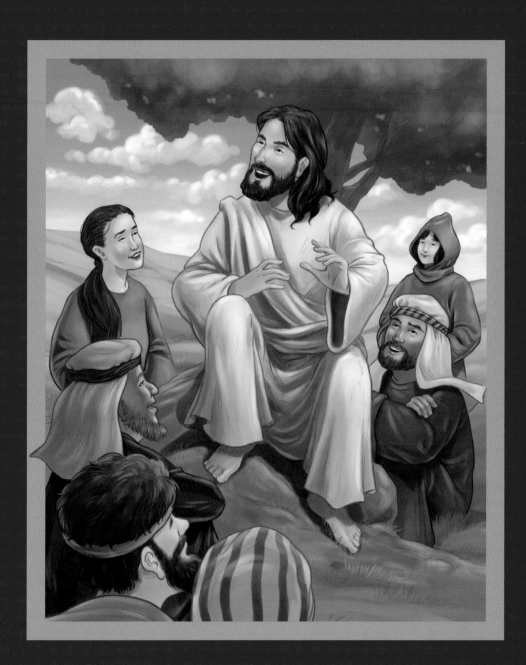

BEYOND THE STORY

The parable of the lost sheep was a story Jesus told to his followers, many of whom were tax collectors and Pharisees. A Pharisee was a member of the Jewish faith that strictly observed all of their religious laws. They felt they were more important than everyone else. Many of them even felt that they did not have to say they were sorry for their sins to God. Jesus used this parable to show them that everyone makes mistakes and everyone sins, and only God will always show us forgiveness and mercy.

In the story, the shepherd realizes that one of his sheep is missing. There is no one nearby he can ask for help. So he has a problem. Does he stay and watch over the 99 sheep with him? Or should he go off and try to find the one that is lost?

The lost sheep represents someone who has sinned against God. We all make mistakes. Like the sheep, sometimes we wander away from what is right and good. Jesus uses the shepherd to represent God. He will always come looking for us and help us find our way back to him. When we seek forgiveness and mercy, we are fixing our relationship with God. He is so excited when a sinner returns to him. Just like the shepherd celebrating with his friends when he finds the lost sheep, God will celebrate with us in heaven for the one sinner who repents. The lesson of the story is that when we make a mistake, we should tell God we are sorry and ask for his forgiveness. Like the shepherd, he will always find us when we are lost.

Mary Berendes has authored dozens of books for children, including nature titles as well as books about countries and holidays. She loves to collect antique books and has some that are almost 200 years old. Mary lives in Minnesota.

Robert Squier has been drawing ever since he could hold a crayon. Today, instead of using crayons, he uses pencils, paint, and the computer. Robert lives in New Hampshire with his wife.